Tunisian Crochet
Baby Blankets

Make 8 beautiful blankets with classic patterns — from cables and ripples to
bobbles and basket weave blocks — using Tunisian crochet, a technique
that combines the look of knitting with the ease of crochet!

2   4   7   10

12   15   18   22

LEISURE ARTS, INC. • Maumelle, Arkansas

Basket Weave Blocks

Blocks of Tunisian Knit Stitches alternate with blocks of Tunisian Purl Stitches to create an attractive basket weave pattern. Stripes produced by solid and heather yarns highlight the blanket.

◼◼◻◻ **EASY**

Finished Size: 33½" x 44¾" (85 cm x 113.5 cm)

SHOPPING LIST

Yarn (Light Weight)

[5 ounces, 362 yards
(140 grams, 331 meters) per skein]:

☐ Blue - 3 skeins

☐ Lt Blue - 3 skeins

Tunisian Hook

Minimum length of 22" (56 cm)

☐ Size K (6.5 mm)

or size needed for gauge

Standard Crochet Hook

☐ Size I (5.5 mm)

GAUGE INFORMATION

With Tunisian hook, in pattern,

16 sts and 14 rows = 4" (10 cm)

STITCH GUIDE

Tunisian Simple Stitch
(Fig. 2, page 29)

Tunisian Knit Stitch
(Fig. 3, page 29)

Tunisian Purl Stitch
(Fig. 4, page 29)

Each row is worked across the length of the Baby Blanket.

INSTRUCTIONS

With Blue and using Tunisian hook, ch 178.

Foundation Row (Right side):
Pull up a loop in horizontal bar of second ch from hook and each ch across, close *(Figs. 1a-c, page 29)*: 178 tss.

Rows 1-4: Skip first vertical bar, (work 4 tps, work 4 tks) across to last st, work tss, close.

Rows 5-8: Skip first vertical bar, (work 4 tks, work 4 tps) across to last st, work tss, close.

Rows 9-19: Repeat Rows 1-8 once, then repeat Rows 1-3 once **more**.

Row 20: Skip first vertical bar, (work 4 tps, work 4 tks) across to last st, work tss, close changing to Lt Blue in last st *(Fig. 10, page 30)*; cut Blue.

Rows 21-24: Skip first vertical bar, (work 4 tks, work 4 tps) across to last st, work tss, close.

Rows 25-32: Repeat Rows 1-8; at end of Row 32, change to Blue in last st; cut Lt Blue.

Rows 33-115: Repeat Rows 1-32 twice, then repeat Rows 1-19 once **more**.

Row 116 (Bind off row)**: With** standard crochet hook, skip first vertical bar, insert hook in next st as for tps, YO and pull up a loop, YO and draw through both loops on hook (**sc made**), inserting hook as for tps, sc in next 3 sts, inserting hook as for tks, sc in next 4 sts, ★ inserting hook as for tps, sc in next 4 sts, inserting hook as for tks, sc in next 4 sts; repeat from ★ across to last st, inserting hook as for tss, sc in last st; finish off.

See Crochet Stitches, pages 30 and 31.

Trim: With right side facing and using standard crochet hook, join Lt Blue with sc in any corner; sc evenly around working 3 sc in each corner; join with slip st to first sc, finish off.

Purple Garden

Variegated yarn brings a breath of spring to this plush wrap worked in Tunisian Full Stitch.

■■□□ **EASY**

Finished Size: 29" x 32" (73.5 cm x 81.5 cm)

SHOPPING LIST

Yarn (Medium Weight) 🄴4

[5 ounces, 230 yards
(141 grams, 211 meters) per skein]:

☐ 5 skeins

Tunisian Hook

Minimum length of 22" (56 cm)

☐ Size K (6.5 mm)

or size needed for gauge

Standard Crochet Hook

☐ Size I (5.5 mm)

GAUGE INFORMATION

With Tunisian hook, in pattern,
15 sts and 17 rows = 4" (10 cm)

── STITCH GUIDE ──

🎥 Tunisian Simple Stitch
(Fig. 2, page 29)

🎥 Tunisian Knit Stitch
(Fig. 3, page 29)

🎥 Tunisian Full Stitch
(Fig. 6, page 30)

INSTRUCTIONS
BODY

With standard crochet hook, ch 106.

🎥 *See Crochet Stitches, pages 30
and 31.*

Row 1 (Right side)**:** Sc in second ch
from hook and in each ch across: 105 sc.

Row 2: Ch 1, turn; sc in each sc across.

Row 3:

Step A (Forward Pass)**:** With Tunisian
hook, ch 1, turn; skip first sc,
★ 🎥 insert hook in next sc *(Fig. A)*,
YO and pull up a loop; repeat from ★
across: 105 loops.

Step B (Return Pass)**:** Do **not** turn;
YO and draw through one loop
on hook *(Fig. 1b, page 29)*, ★ YO
and draw through 2 loops on hook
(Fig. 1c, page 29); repeat from ★
across until one loop remains on
hook: 105 tss.

Fig. A

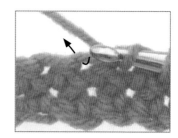

Row 4: Skip first vertical bar, work tfs across to last horizontal bar, skip last horizontal bar, work tss, close: 103 tfs and 2 tss.

Row 5: Skip first 2 vertical bars, work tfs across to last st, work tss, close: 103 tfs and 2 tss.

Rows 6-130: Repeat Rows 4 and 5, 62 times; then repeat Row 4 once **more**: 103 tfs and 2 tss.

Row 131: With standard crochet hook, skip first vertical bar, working in sps **between** tfs, ★ insert hook in next sp, YO and pull up a loop, YO and draw through both loops on hook (**sc made**); repeat from ★ across to last st, inserting hook as for tss, sc in last st: 105 sc.

Row 132: Ch 1, turn; sc in each sc across; do **not** finish off.

EDGING

Rnd 1: Ch 1, turn; 🎥 sc evenly around working 3 sc in each corner; join with slip st to first sc.

Rnd 2: Ch 1, do **not** turn; 🎥 working from **left** to **right**, insert hook in st to **right** of hook (*Fig. B*), YO and draw through, under and to left of loop on hook (2 loops on hook) (*Fig. C*), YO and draw through both loops on hook (*Fig. D*) (*reverse sc made, Fig. E*); join with slip st to first st, finish off.

Fig. B

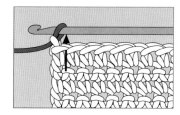

Fig. C

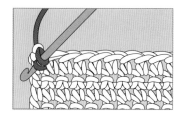

Fig. D

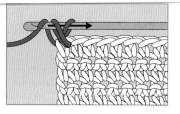

Fig. E

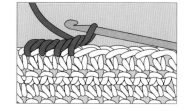

Frosted Stitch Stripes

Clusters create little peaks that alternate with Tunisian Simple Stitches to produce this textured stitch pattern. The fringe combines both stripe colors to give the blanket a polished finish.

◨■▢▢ **EASY**

Finished Size: 30" x 34" (76 cm x 86.5 cm)

Shown on page 9.

INSTRUCTIONS
BODY

With Green and using Tunisian hook, ch 135.

Foundation Row (Right side):
Step A (Forward Pass): Pull up a loop in horizontal bar of second ch from hook and each ch across *(Fig. 1a, page 29)*: 135 loops.
Step B (Return Pass): Do **not** turn; YO and draw though one loop on hook *(Fig. 1b, page 29)*, [YO and draw through 2 loops on hook *(Fig. 1c, page 29)*] twice, ★ ch 1 *(Fig. A)*, YO and draw through 4 loops on hook (**Cluster made**) *(Fig. B)*, ch 1, (YO and draw through 2 loops on hook) 3 times; repeat from ★ across until one loop remains: 22 Clusters, 44 ch-1 sps, and 69 tss.

Fig. A

Fig. B

Rows 1-9:
Step A (Forward Pass): Skip first vertical bar, work 2 tss, ★ insert hook in next ch-1 sp, YO and pull up a loop, insert hook in horizontal bar on top of next Cluster, YO and pull up a loop, insert hook in next ch-1 sp, YO and pull up a loop, work 3 tss; repeat from ★ across: 135 loops.
Step B (Return Pass): Do **not** turn; YO and draw though one loop on hook, (YO and draw through 2 loops on hook) twice, ★ ch 1, YO and draw through 4 loops on hook (**Cluster made**), ch 1, (YO and draw through 2 loops on hook) 3 times; repeat from ★ across; at end of Row 9, change to Yellow in last st *(Fig. 10, page 30)*, cut Green: 22 Clusters, 44 ch-1 sps, and 69 tss.

7

Rows 10-19: With Yellow, repeat Row 1, 10 times; at end of Row 19, change to Green in last st, cut Yellow.

Rows 20-29: With Green, repeat Row 1, 10 times; at end of Row 29, change to Yellow in last st, drop Green.

Do **not** cut yarn unless instructed. Carry unused yarn **loosely** along the edge.

Rows 30 and 31: With Yellow, repeat Row 1 twice; at end of Row 31, change to Green in last st, drop Yellow.

Row 32: With Green, repeat Row 1, changing to Yellow in last st; drop Green.

Rows 33-82: Repeat Rows 30-32, 16 times; then repeat Rows 30 and 31 once **more**; at end of Row 82, cut Yellow.

Rows 83-92: With Green, repeat Row 1, 10 times; at end of Row 92, change to Yellow in last st, cut Green.

Rows 93-102: With Yellow, repeat Row 1, 10 times; at end of Row 102, change to Green in last st, cut Yellow.

Rows 103-110: With Green, repeat Row 1, 8 times; at end of Row 110, do **not** change color.

🎬 *See Crochet Stitches, pages 30 and 31.*

Row 111 (Bind off row): With standard crochet hook, ch 1, skip first vertical bar, insert hook in next st as for tss, YO and pull up a loop, YO and draw through both loops on hook (**sc made**), sc in next st as for tss, sc in next ch-1 sp, sc in horizontal bar on top of next Cluster, sc in next ch-1 sp, ★ sc in next 3 sts as for tss, sc in next ch-1 sp, sc in next horizontal bar on top of next Cluster, sc in next ch-1 sp; repeat from ★ across to last 3 sts, inserting hook as for tss, sc in next 2 sts, slip st in last st; finish off.

FRINGE

Cut a piece of cardboard 5" wide x 6" long (12.5 cm x 15 cm). Holding one strand of each color together, wind the yarn **loosely** and **evenly** lengthwise around the cardboard until the card is filled, then cut across one end; repeat as needed.

Hold 3 strands of each color together; fold in half. With **wrong** side of short edge facing, draw the folded end up through a second stitch and pull the loose ends through the folded end *(Fig. C)*; draw the knot up **tightly** *(Fig. D)*. Repeat across each short edge, skipping 2 sts between each fringe and leaving last vertical bar unworked. Lay Blanket flat on a hard surface and trim the ends.

Fig. C

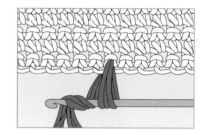

Fig. D

Color Waves

A contemporary color palette brings bold movement to rippling chevrons worked in Tunisian Simple Stitch.

■■□□ **EASY**

Finished Size: 33¼" x 39½" (84.5 cm x 100.5 cm)

SHOPPING LIST

Yarn (Medium Weight)

[5 ounces, 256 yards
(141 grams, 234 meters) per skein]:

☐ Green - 2 skeins

☐ White - 2 skeins

☐ Purple - 2 skeins

☐ Lt Purple - 2 skeins

Tunisian Hook

Minimum length of 22" (56 cm)

☐ Size K (6.5 mm)

   or size needed for gauge

Standard Crochet Hook

☐ Size H (5 mm)

GAUGE INFORMATION

With Tunisian hook, in pattern,

   12 sts (one repeat) = 2¾" (7 cm);

   10 rows = 4" (10 cm)

—— STITCH GUIDE ——

Tunisian Simple Stitch
   (Fig. 2, page 29)

Make One *(Fig. 9, page 30)*

Decrease (uses 3 loops)

Work 3 tss, YO and draw through
3 loops on hook (2 sts decreased).

INSTRUCTIONS

With Green and using Tunisian hook,
ch 145.

Foundation Row (Right side):

Pull up a loop in horizontal bar
of second ch from hook and each
ch across, close *(Figs. 1a-c, page 29)*:
145 tss.

Rows 1-3: ★ M1, work 4 tss, decrease,
(2 sts decreased), work 4 tss, M1, work
tss; repeat from ★ across, close.

Row 4: ★ M1, work 4 tss, decrease,
work 4 tss, M1, work tss; repeat from
★ across, close changing to White
in last st *(Fig. 10, page 30)*; cut Green.

Rows 5-8: ★ M1, work 4 tss, decrease, work 4 tss, M1, work tss; repeat from ★ across, close.

Row 9: ★ M1, work 4 tss, decrease, work 4 tss, M1, work tss; repeat from ★ across, close changing to Purple in last st; cut White.

Rows 10-14: Repeat Rows 5-9; at end of Row 14, change to Lt Purple in last st; cut Purple.

Rows 15-19: Repeat Rows 5-9; at end of Row 19, change to Green in last st; cut Lt Purple.

Rows 20-24: Repeat Rows 5-9; at end of Row 24, change to White in last st; cut Green.

Rows 25-98: Repeat Rows 5-24, 3 times; then repeat Rows 5-18 once **more**.

Row 99 (Bind off row)**:** With standard crochet hook, skip first vertical bar, ★ insert hook in next st as for tss, YO and pull up a loop, YO and draw through both loops on hook (**sc made**); repeat from ★ across; finish off.

Bubbling Bobbles

Bobbles are just plain fun — for you to crochet and for baby to touch!

⬛⬛⬛⬜ **INTERMEDIATE**

Finished Size: 33" (84 cm) square

SHOPPING LIST

Yarn (Medium Weight)

[5 ounces, 256 yards
(141 grams, 234 meters) per skein]:

☐ White - 3 skeins

☐ Yellow - 3 skeins

☐ Green - 3 skeins

Tunisian Hook

Minimum length of 22" (56 cm)

☐ Size K (6.5 mm)

or size needed for gauge

Standard Crochet Hook

☐ Size H (5 mm)

GAUGE INFORMATION

With Tunisian hook, in pattern,
16 sts and 10 rows = 4" (10 cm)

——— STITCH GUIDE ———

🎥 Tunisian Simple Stitch
(Fig. 2, page 29)

🎥 Tunisian Double Stitch
(Figs. 7a & b, page 30)

🎥 Tunisian Bobble Stitch
(Figs. 8a & b, page 30)

INSTRUCTIONS

With White and using Tunisian hook,
ch 131.

Foundation Row (Right side):
🎥 Pull up a loop in horizontal bar
of second ch from hook and each
ch across, close *(Figs. 1a-c, page 29)*:
131 tss.

Rows 1 and 2: Skip first vertical bar,
work tss across, close.

Row 3: Skip first vertical bar, work tss
across, close 🎥 changing to Yellow
in last st *(Fig. 10, page 30)*; cut White.

Row 4: Skip first vertical bar, work 8 tss, work tbs, ★ work 3 tss, work tbs; repeat from ★ across to last 9 sts, work 9 tss, close: 29 tbs and 102 tss.

Row 5: Skip first vertical bar, work tss across, close changing to Green in last st; cut Yellow: 131 tss.

Row 6: Skip first vertical bar, work 6 tss, work tbs, ★ work 3 tss, work tbs; repeat from ★ across to last 7 sts, work 7 tss, close: 30 tbs and 101 tss.

Row 7: Skip first vertical bar, work tss across, close changing to White in last st; cut Green: 131 tss.

Row 8: Skip first vertical bar, work 8 tss, work tbs, ★ work 3 tss, work tbs; repeat from ★ across to last 9 sts, work 9 tss, close: 29 tbs and 102 tss.

Row 9: Skip first vertical bar, work tss across, close changing to Yellow in last st; cut White: 131 tss.

Row 10: Skip first vertical bar, work 6 tss, work tbs, ★ work 3 tss, work tbs; repeat from ★ across to last 7 sts, work 7 tss, close: 30 tbs and 101 tss.

Row 11: Skip first vertical bar, work tss across, close changing to Green in last st; cut Yellow: 131 tss.

Row 12: Skip first vertical bar, work 8 tss, work tbs, ★ work 3 tss, work tbs; repeat from ★ across to last 9 sts, work 9 tss, close: 29 tbs and 102 tss.

Row 13: Skip first vertical bar, work tss across, close changing to White in last st; cut Green: 131 tss.

Row 14: Skip first vertical bar, work 6 tss, work tbs, ★ work 3 tss, work tbs; repeat from ★ across to last 7 sts, work 7 tss, close: 30 tbs and 101 tss.

Row 15: Skip first vertical bar, work tss across, close changing to Yellow in last st; cut White: 131 tss.

Rows 16-79: Repeat Rows 4-15, 5 times; then repeat Rows 4-7 once **more**: 131 tss.

Rows 80 and 81: Skip first vertical bar, work tss across, close.

Row 82 (Bind off row)**:** With standard crochet hook, skip first vertical bar, ★ insert hook in next vertical bar as for tss, YO and pull up a loop, YO and draw through 2 loops on hook (**sc made**); repeat from ★ across; finish off.

See Crochet Stitches, pages 30 and 31.

Trim: With **wrong** side facing and using standard crochet hook, join Yellow with sc in any corner; sc evenly around working 3 sc in each corner; join with slip st to first sc, finish off.

Telegram

Showcasing Tunisian Extended Stitch, dots and dashes in blue and white send a beautiful message.

⬤⬛⬛◻ **INTERMEDIATE**

Finished Size: 34¾" x 42½" (88.5 cm x 108 cm)

Shown on page 17.

SHOPPING LIST

Yarn (Light Weight)

[5 ounces, 358 yards
(141 grams, 328 meters) per skein]:

☐ White - 3 skeins

☐ Blue - 2 skeins

Tunisian Hook

Minimum length of 22" (56 cm)

☐ Size K (6.5 mm)

  or size needed for gauge

Standard Crochet Hook

☐ Size H (5 mm)

GAUGE INFORMATION

With Tunisian hook, in pattern,

  16 sts and 12 rows = 4" (10 cm)

—— STITCH GUIDE ——

🎥 Tunisian Simple Stitch

  (Fig. 2, page 29)

🎥 Tunisian Extended Stitch

  (Fig. 5, page 29)

INSTRUCTIONS

BODY

With White and using Tunisian hook, ch 130.

Foundation Row (Right side):

🎥 Working in horizontal bars of chs *(Fig. A)*, pull up a loop in third ch from hook, ch 1 *(Fig. B)*, ★ pull up a loop in next ch, ch 1; repeat from ★ across,

🎥 close *(Figs. 1b & c, page 29)*

🎥 changing to Blue in last st *(Fig. 10, page 30)*; drop White: 129 sts.

Fig. A

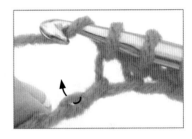

Fig. B

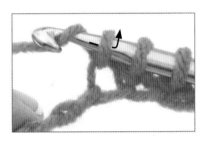

Do **not** cut yarn unless instructed. Carry unused yarn **loosely** along the edge.

On a Weaving row, you will be holding the working yarn to the **front** or to the **back** as you slip the vertical bars onto the hook.

Row 1 (Weaving row)**:** With Blue, skip first vertical bar, slip next vertical bar onto hook, ★ 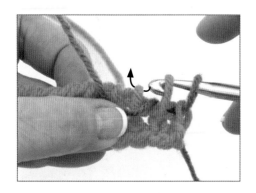 with yarn in **front**, slip next vertical bar onto hook *(Fig. C)*,  with yarn in **back**, slip next vertical bar onto hook *(Fig. D)*; repeat from ★ across to last st, with yarn in **front**, work tss, close.

Fig. C

Fig. D

When working the row following a Weaving row, insert hook in vertical bar above the woven strand to work tes.

Row 2: Ch 1, skip first vertical bar, work tes across, close changing to White in last st; drop Blue.

Row 3 (Weaving row)**:** With White, skip first vertical bar, with yarn in **front**, slip next vertical bar onto hook, ★ with yarn in **back**, slip next vertical bar onto hook, with yarn in **front**, slip next vertical bar onto hook; repeat from ★ across to last st, work tss, close.

Row 4: Ch 1, skip first vertical bar, work tes across, close changing to Blue in last st; drop White.

Row 5 (Weaving row)**:** With Blue, skip first vertical bar, slip next vertical bar onto hook, ★ with yarn in **front**, slip next vertical bar onto hook, with yarn in **back**, slip next vertical bar onto hook; repeat from ★ across to last st, with yarn in **front**, work tss, close.

Rows 6-119: Repeat Rows 2-5, 28 times; then repeat Rows 2 and 3 once **more**; at the end of Row 119, cut Blue.

Row 120 (Bind off row)**:** With standard crochet hook, ch 1, skip first vertical bar, ★  insert hook in next st as for tss, YO and pull up a loop, YO and draw through one loop on hook, YO and draw through both loops on hook **(ex sc made)**; repeat from ★ across; do **not** finish off.

EDGING

See Crochet Stitches, pages 30 and 31.

Rnd 1: With standard crochet hook, ch 2 (**counts as first hdc**), turn; hdc evenly around working 3 hdc in each corner; join with slip st to first hdc.

Rnd 2: Ch 3 (**counts as first dc**), turn; dc in next hdc and in each hdc around working 3 dc in center hdc of each corner 3-hdc group; join with slip st to first dc.

Rnd 3: Ch 3 (**counts as first dc**), turn; dc in next dc and in each dc around working 3 dc in center dc of each corner 3-dc group; join with slip st to first dc, finish off.

Rnd 4: With **right** side facing and using standard crochet hook, join Blue with sc in center dc of any corner 3-dc group; 2 sc in same st, sc in each dc around working 3 sc in center dc of each corner 3-dc group; join with slip st to first sc, finish off.

Cables & Honeycombs

Cables in Tunisian crochet are easier than they look! Front and Back Cables frame Tunisian Simple Stitch, which in turn encloses a central honeycomb panel of Tunisian Knit and Purl Stitches. Worked in ivory and topped off with a quartet of big corner tassels, this blanket is a classic.

◖■■■▢ INTERMEDIATE

Finished Size: 31½" x 34" (80 cm x 86.5 cm)

SHOPPING LIST

Yarn (Medium Weight)

[3.5 ounces, 170 yards
(100 grams, 156 meters) per skein]:

☐ 7 skeins

Tunisian Hook

Minimum length of 22" (56 cm)

☐ Size K (6.5 mm)

or size needed for gauge

Standard Crochet Hook

☐ Size I (5.5 mm)

Additional Supplies

☐ Cable needle

☐ Yarn needle

GAUGE INFORMATION

With Tunisian hook, in tps,

16 sts and 13 rows = 4" (10 cm)

─── STITCH GUIDE ───

Tunisian Simple Stitch
(Fig. 2, page 29)

Tunisian Knit Stitch
(Fig. 3, page 29)

Tunisian Purl Stitch
(Fig. 4, page 29)

Back Cable (uses 6 sts)

Work 3 tks **loosely**, slip 3 tks just made onto a cable needle and hold at **back** *(Fig. A)*, work 3 tks **loosely**, slip 3 tks from cable needle onto hook *(Fig. B)*.

Fig. A

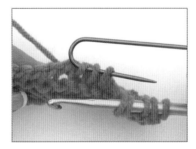

Fig. B

Front Cable (uses 6 sts)

Work 3 tks **loosely**, slip 3 tks just made onto a cable needle and hold at **front** *(Fig. C)*, work 3 tks **loosely**, slip 3 tks from cable needle onto hook *(Fig. D)*.

Fig. C

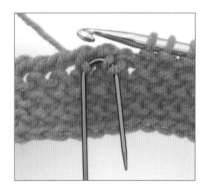

Fig. D

INSTRUCTIONS
BODY

With Tunisian hook, ch 126.

Foundation Row (Right side):

Pull up a loop in horizontal bar of second ch from hook and each ch across, close *(Figs. 1a-c, page 29)*: 126 tss.

Rows 1-3: Skip first vertical bar, work tps across to last st, work tss, close.

When working the closing across the Cables, pull the loops apart as you work, being careful to draw through 2 loops at a time not 3.

Row 4: Skip first vertical bar, (work 4 tps, work Back Cable) 6 times, work 4 tps, (work Front Cable, work 4 tps) 6 times, work tss, close: 12 Cables, 52 tps, and 2 tss.

Rows 5-7: Skip first vertical bar, work 4 tps, (work 6 tks, work 4 tps) across to last st, work tss, close: 72 tks, 52 tps, and 2 tss.

Rows 8-15: Repeat Rows 4-7 twice.

Row 16: Skip first vertical bar, (work 4 tps, work Back Cable) twice, work 84 tps, (work Front Cable, work 4 tps) twice, work tss, close: 4 Cables, 100 tps, and 2 tss.

Rows 17-19: Skip first vertical bar, (work 4 tps, work 6 tks) twice, work 84 tps, (work 6 tks, work 4 tps) twice, work tss, close: 24 tks, 100 tps, and 2 tss.

Row 20: Skip first vertical bar, work 4 tps, (work Back Cable, work 4 tps) twice, work 76 tss, work 4 tps, (work Front Cable, work 4 tps) twice, work tss: 4 Cables, 24 tps, and 78 tss.

Rows 21-23: Skip first vertical bar, work 4 tps, (work 6 tks, work 4 tps) twice, work 76 tss, work 4 tps, (work 6 tks, work 4 tps) twice, work tss: 24 tks, 24 tps, and 78 tss.

Rows 24-31: Repeat Rows 20-23 twice.

Row 32: Skip first vertical bar, work 4 tps, (work Back Cable, work 4 tps) twice, work 12 tss, (work tps, work tss) 26 times, work 12 tss, work 4 tps, (work Front Cable, work 4 tps) twice, work tss: 4 Cables, 50 tps, and 52 tss.

Row 33: Skip first vertical bar, work 4 tps, (work 6 tks, work 4 tps) twice, work 12 tss, (work tss, work tps) 26 times, work 12 tss, work 4 tps, (work 6 tks, work 4 tps) twice, work tss: 24 tks, 50 tps, and 52 tss.

Row 34: Skip first vertical bar, work 4 tps, (work 6 tks, work 4 tps) twice, work 12 tss, (work tps, work tss) 26 times, work 12 tss, work 4 tps, (work 6 tks, work 4 tps) twice, work tss: 24 tks, 50 tps, and 52 tss.

Row 35: Skip first vertical bar, work 4 tps, (work 6 tks, work 4 tps) twice, work 12 tss, (work tss, work tps) 26 times, work 12 tss, work 4 tps, (work 6 tks, work 4 tps) twice, work tss: 24 tks, 50 tps, and 52 tss.

Rows 36-79: Repeat Rows 32-35, 11 times.

Rows 80-91: Repeat Rows 20-23, 3 times.

Rows 92-95: Repeat Rows 16-19.

Rows 96-107: Repeat Rows 4-7, 3 times.

Rows 108-110: Repeat Rows 1-3.

Row 111 (Bind off row)**:** With standard crochet hook, skip first vertical bar, ★ insert hook in next st as for tps, YO and pull up a loop, YO and draw through both loops on hook (**sc made**); repeat from ★ across to last st, inserting hook as for tss, sc in last st; finish off.

TASSEL (Make 4)

Cut a piece of cardboard 3" wide x 7" long (7.5 cm x 18 cm). Wind a double strand of yarn around the cardboard approximately 15 times. Cut an 18" (45.5 cm) length of yarn and insert it under all of the strands at the top of the cardboard; pull up **tightly** and tie securely. Leave the yarn ends long enough to attach the tassel. Cut the yarn at the opposite end of the cardboard *(Fig. E)* and then remove it. Cut a 6" (15 cm) length of yarn and wrap it **tightly** around the tassel twice, 1" (2.5 cm) below the top *(Fig. F)*; tie securely. Trim the ends.

Attach one Tassel to each corner of Blanket.

Fig. E

Fig. F

Bright Strands

Stranded colorwork, using two colors in any given row, brings vibrance to this blanket worked in Tunisian Simple Stitch. The working color is pulled up in the right spot to match the geometric pattern, with the unused color carried across the back. Follow the chart and you'll get the hang of this interesting technique in no time.

◖◼◼◻◻ **INTERMEDIATE +**

Finished Size: 30" x 42½" (76 cm x 108 cm)

SHOPPING LIST

Yarn (Medium Weight) 🧶 **4**

[3.5 ounces, 190 yards
(100 grams, 174 meters) per skein]:

☐ White - 4 skeins

☐ Blue - 3 skeins

☐ Yellow - 2 skeins

Tunisian Hook

Minimum length of 22" (56 cm)

☐ Size K (6.5 mm)

or size needed for gauge

Standard Crochet Hook

☐ Size I (5.5 mm)

GAUGE INFORMATION

With Tunisian hook, 15 tss and
10 rows = 4" (10 cm)

──── STITCH GUIDE ────

 Tunisian Simple Stitch
(Fig. 2, page 29)

PRACTICE SWATCH

Finished Size: 8½"w x 5¼"h
(21.5 cm x 13.25 cm)

The pattern is a multiple of 8 sts.

Work the Practice Swatch to get comfortable with changing colors and stranding the yarn.

With White and using Tunisian hook, ch 32.

Foundation Row (Right side):

 Pull up a loop in horizontal bar of second ch from hook and each ch across, close *(Figs. 1a-c, page 29)*: 32 tss.

Row 1: Skip first vertical bar, work tss across, close 🎥 changing to Blue in last st *(Fig. 10, page 30)*.

Color Pattern: Work same as Rows 1-13 of Body, page 24, **or** follow Chart A, page 27 for 13 rows; cut Blue and finish off White.

INSTRUCTIONS
BOTTOM BORDER

With White and using Tunisian hook, ch 112.

Foundation Row (Right side):
🎥 Pull up a loop in horizontal bar of second ch from hook and each ch across, close *(Figs. 1a-c, page 29)*: 112 tss.

Row 1: Skip first vertical bar, work tss across, close 🎥 changing to Blue in last st *(Fig. 10, page 30)*.

BODY

If desired, you can follow chart instructions for the Body on page 26.

Do **not** cut yarn unless instructed.
🎥 Carry unused yarn **loosely** across **wrong** side *(Fig. A)*. When closing,
🎥 change to next color when one loop of the previous color remains on the hook *(Fig. B)*.
When the first stitch on the next row is a different color than the last stitch on the closing, complete the last stitch with the first color of the next row.

Fig. A

Fig. B

Row 1:

Step A (Forward Pass): Skip first vertical bar, with White, work 2 tss, drop White, with Blue, work 3 tss, drop Blue, with White, work 2 tss, ★ drop White, with Blue, work tss, drop Blue, with White, work 2 tss, drop White, with Blue, work 3 tss, drop Blue, with White, work 2 tss; repeat from ★ across.

Step B (Return Pass): With White, YO and draw through one loop on hook, YO and draw through 2 loops on hook, drop White, (with Blue, YO and draw through 2 loops on hook) 3 times, drop Blue, (with White, YO and draw through 2 loops on hook) twice, drop White, with Blue, YO and draw through 2 loops on hook, ★ drop Blue, (with White, YO and draw through 2 loops on hook) twice, drop White, (with Blue, YO and draw through 2 loops on hook) 3 times, drop Blue, (with White, YO and draw through 2 loops on hook) twice, drop White, with Blue, YO and draw through 2 loops on hook; repeat from ★ across.

TIP: If desired, you may want to line the afghan with a soft flannel fabric to ensure baby does not hang little fingers or toes on the floats.

Continue to change colors in same manner.

Row 2: Skip first vertical bar, with Blue, work tss, with White, work 2 tss, with Blue, work tss, with White, work 2 tss, ★ with Blue, work 3 tss, with White, work 2 tss, with Blue, work tss, with White, work 2 tss; repeat from ★ across to last st, with Blue, work tss, close changing to White in last st.

Row 3: Skip first vertical bar, with Blue, work 2 tss, with White, work 3 tss, with Blue, work 2 tss, ★ with White, work tss, with Blue, work 2 tss, with White, work 3 tss, with Blue, work 2 tss; repeat from ★ across, close.

Row 4: Skip first vertical bar, with Blue, work 3 tss, ★ with White, work tss, with Blue, work 3 tss; repeat from ★ across, close.

Row 5: Skip first vertical bar, with Blue, work 2 tss, with White, work 3 tss, with Blue, work 2 tss, ★ with White, work tss, with Blue, work 2 tss, with White, work 3 tss, with Blue, work 2 tss; repeat from ★ across, close changing to Blue in last st.

Row 6: Skip first vertical bar, with Blue, work tss, with White, work 2 tss, with Blue, work tss, with White, work 2 tss, ★ with Blue, work 3 tss, with White, work 2 tss, with Blue, work tss, with White, work 2 tss; repeat from ★ across to last st, with Blue, work tss, close.

Row 7: Skip first vertical bar, with White, work 2 tss, with Blue, work 3 tss, with White, work 2 tss, ★ with Blue, work tss, with White, work 2 tss, with Blue, work 3 tss, with White, work 2 tss; repeat from ★ across, close changing to White in last st.

Row 8: Skip first vertical bar, with White, work tss, with Blue, work 2 tss, with White, work tss, with Blue, work 2 tss, ★ with White, work 3 tss, with Blue, work 2 tss, with White, work tss, with Blue, work 2 tss; repeat from ★ across to last st, with White, work tss, close.

Row 9: Skip first vertical bar, with Blue, work 3 tss, ★ with White, work tss, with Blue, work 3 tss; repeat from ★ across, close.

Row 10: Skip first vertical bar, with White, work tss, with Blue, work 2 tss, with White, work tss, with Blue, work 2 tss, ★ with White, work 3 tss, with Blue, work 2 tss, with White, work tss, with Blue, work 2 tss; repeat from ★ across to last st, with White, work tss, close changing to Blue in last st.

Row 11: Skip first vertical bar, with White, work 2 tss, with Blue, work 3 tss, with White, work 2 tss, ★ with Blue, work tss, with White, work 2 tss, with Blue, work 3 tss, with White, work 2 tss; repeat from ★ across, close.

Row 12: Skip first vertical bar, with Blue, work tss, with White, work 2 tss, with Blue, work tss, with White, work 2 tss, ★ with Blue, work 3 tss, with White, work 2 tss, with Blue, work tss, with White, work 2 tss; repeat from ★ across to last st, with Blue, work tss, close changing to White in last st.

Row 13: Skip first vertical bar, with Blue, work 2 tss, with White, work 3 tss, with Blue, work 2 tss, ★ with White, work tss, with Blue, work 2 tss, with White, work 3 tss, with Blue, work 2 tss; repeat from ★ across, close.

Cut Blue.

Rows 14-26: Substituting Yellow for Blue, repeat Rows 4-13 once, then repeat Rows 4-6 once **more**; at end of Row 26, cut Yellow.

Rows 27-30: Repeat Rows 7-10.

Rows 31-76: Repeat Rows 1-10, 4 times; then repeat Rows 1-6 once **more**; at end of Row 76, cut Blue.

Rows 77-83: Substituting Yellow for Blue, repeat Rows 7-13.

Rows 84-89: Substituting Yellow for Blue, repeat Rows 4-9; at end of Row 89, cut Yellow.

Row 90: Repeat Row 10.

Rows 91-102: Repeat Rows 1-12; at end of Row 102, cut Blue.

TOP BORDER

Row 1: Skip first vertical bar, work tss across, close.

Row 2 (Bind off row): With standard crochet hook, skip first vertical bar, ★ insert hook in next vertical bar as for tss, YO and pull up a loop, YO and draw through 2 loops on hook (**sc made**); repeat from ★ across; finish off.

See Crochet Stitches, pages 30 and 31.

Trim: With **right** side facing and using standard crochet hook, join Yellow with sc in any corner; sc evenly around working 3 sc in each corner; join with slip st to first sc, finish off.

CHART INSTRUCTIONS
BODY
FOLLOWING A CHART

The unworked vertical bar on the right edge of each row is the first stitch on the chart.
Each row is worked in two parts forward pass and close (return pass). Follow stitch repeat across each row.

CHANGING COLORS

Do **not** cut yarn unless instructed. Carry unused yarn **loosely** across **wrong** side *(Fig. A, page 24)*. On forward pass, pull up the color yarn that matches the chart; on closing (return pass), change to next color when one loop of the previous color remains on the hook *(Fig. B, page 24)*. When the first stitch on the next row is a different color than the last stitch on the closing, complete the last stitch with the first color of the next row.

Rows 1-26: Follow Chart A on page 27; at end of Row 26, cut Yellow.

Rows 27-76: Follow Chart B on page 27, Rows 27-36, 5 times; at end of Row 76, cut Blue.

Rows 77-102: Follow Chart C on page 27; at end of Row 102, cut Blue.

Work Top Border and Trim.

Chart A

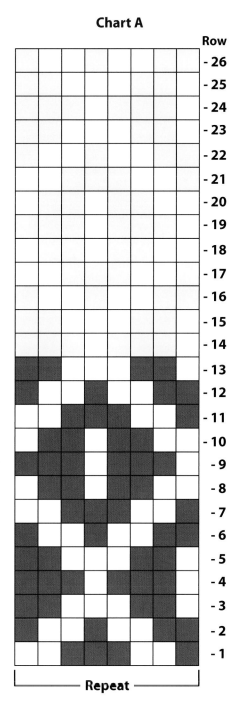

Row
- 26
- 25
- 24
- 23
- 22
- 21
- 20
- 19
- 18
- 17
- 16
- 15
- 14
- 13
- 12
- 11
- 10
- 9
- 8
- 7
- 6
- 5
- 4
- 3
- 2
- 1

└── **Repeat** ──┘

Chart B

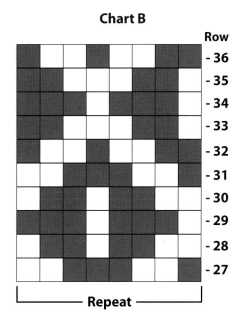

Row
- 36
- 35
- 34
- 33
- 32
- 31
- 30
- 29
- 28
- 27

└── **Repeat** ──┘

Chart C

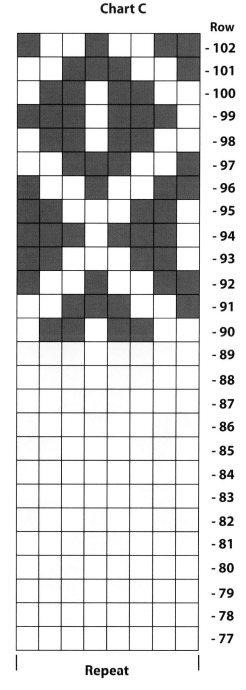

Row
- 102
- 101
- 100
- 99
- 98
- 97
- 96
- 95
- 94
- 93
- 92
- 91
- 90
- 89
- 88
- 87
- 86
- 85
- 84
- 83
- 82
- 81
- 80
- 79
- 78
- 77

└── **Repeat** ──┘

General Instructions

ABBREVIATIONS

ch(s)	chain(s)
cm	centimeters
dc	double crochet(s)
ex sc	extended single crochet(s)
hdc	half double crochet(s)
M1	Make One
mm	millimeters
Rnd(s)	Round(s)
sc	single crochet(s)
sp(s)	space(s)
st(s)	stitch(es)
tbs	Tunisian Bobble Stitch
tds	Tunisian Double Stitch
tes	Tunisian Extended Stitch
tfs	Tunisian Full Stitch
tks	Tunisian Knit Stitch
tps	Tunisian Purl Stitch
tss	Tunisian Simple Stitch
YO	yarn over

CROCHET TERMINOLOGY

UNITED STATES		INTERNATIONAL
slip stitch (slip st)	=	single crochet (sc)
single crochet (sc)	=	double crochet (dc)
half double crochet (hdc)	=	half treble crochet (htr)
double crochet (dc)	=	treble crochet(tr)
treble crochet (tr)	=	double treble crochet (dtr)
double treble crochet (dtr)	=	triple treble crochet (ttr)
triple treble crochet (tr tr)	=	quadruple treble crochet (qtr)
skip	=	miss

SYMBOLS & TERMS

★ — work instructions following ★ as many **more** times as indicated in addition to the first time.

( ) or [ ] — work enclosed instructions **as many** times as specified by the number immediately following **or** contains explanatory remarks.

colon (:) — the number(s) given after a colon at the end of a row denote(s) the number of stitches you should have on that row.

GAUGE

Exact gauge is **essential** for proper size. Before beginning your project, make a sample swatch in the yarn and hook specified in the individual instructions. After completing the swatch, measure it, counting your stitches and rows carefully. If the swatch is larger/smaller than specified, **make another, changing hook size to get the correct gauge.** Keep trying until you find the size hook that will give you the specified gauge.

Yarn Weight Symbol & Names	LACE 0	SUPER FINE 1	FINE 2	LIGHT 3	MEDIUM 4	BULKY 5	SUPER BULKY 6
Type of Yarns in Category	Fingering, 10-count crochet thread	Sock, Fingering Baby	Sport, Baby	DK, Light Worsted	Worsted, Afghan, Aran	Chunky, Craft, Rug	Bulky, Roving
Crochet Gauge* Ranges in Single Crochet to 4" (10 cm)	32-42 double crochets**	21-32 sts	16-20 sts	12-17 sts	11-14 sts	8-11 sts	5-9 sts
Advised Hook Size Range	Steel*** 6,7,8 Regular hook B-1	B-1 to E-4	E-4 to 7	7 to I-9	I-9 to K-10.5	K-10.5 to M-13	M-13 and larger

*GUIDELINES ONLY: The chart above reflects the most commonly used gauges and hook sizes for specific yarn categories.

** Lace weight yarns are usually crocheted on larger-size hooks to create lacy openwork patterns. Accordingly, a gauge range is difficult to determine. Always follow the gauge stated in your pattern.

*** Steel crochet hooks are sized differently from regular hooks–the higher the number the smaller the hook, which is the reverse of regular hook sizing.

CROCHET HOOKS

U.S.	B-1	C-2	D-3	E-4	F-5	G-6	H-8	I-9	J-10	K-10½	L-11	M/N-13	N/P-15	P/Q	Q	S
Metric - mm	2.25	2.75	3.25	3.5	3.75	4	5	5.5	6	6.5	8	9	10	15	16	19

◼◻◻◻ BEGINNER	Projects for first-time crocheters using basic stitches. Minimal shaping.
◼◼◻◻ EASY	Projects using yarn with basic stitches, repetitive stitch patterns, simple color changes, and simple shaping and finishing.
◼◼◼◻ INTERMEDIATE	Projects using a variety of techniques, such as basic lace patterns or color patterns, mid-level shaping and finishing.
◼◼◼◼ EXPERIENCED	Projects with intricate stitch patterns, techniques and dimension, such as non-repeating patterns, multi-color techniques, fine threads, small hooks, detailed shaping and refined finishing.

FOUNDATION ROW

Chain the number indicated in the pattern.

Forward Pass: Pull up a loop in horizontal bar of second ch from hook and each ch across *(Fig. 1a)*.

To Close (Return Pass)**:** YO and draw through one loop on hook **(ch 1 made)** *(Fig. 1b)*, (YO and draw through 2 loops on hook) across *(Fig. 1c)*: one loop.

Fig. 1a

Fig. 1b

Fig. 1c

TUNISIAN SIMPLE STITCH *(abbreviated tss)*

Insert hook from **right** to **left** under next vertical bar *(Fig. 2)*, YO and pull up a loop.

Fig. 2

TUNISIAN KNIT STITCH *(abbreviated tks)*

Insert hook from **front** to **back** between front and back vertical bars of next stitch *(Fig. 3)*, YO and pull up a loop.

Fig. 3

TUNISIAN PURL STITCH *(abbreviated tps)*

With yarn in **front** of work, insert hook from **right** to **left** under next vertical bar *(Fig. 4)*, YO and pull up a loop.

Fig. 4

TUNISIAN EXTENDED STITCH *(abbreviated tes)*

Insert hook from **front** to **back** under next vertical bar, YO and pull up a loop, [YO *(Fig. 5)* and draw through one loop on hook **(ch 1 made)**].

Fig. 5

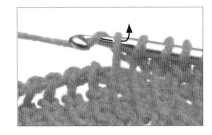

TUNISIAN FULL STITCH
(abbreviated tfs)

Insert hook from **front** to **back** under horizontal bar between two stitches *(Fig. 6)*, YO and pull up a loop.

Fig. 6

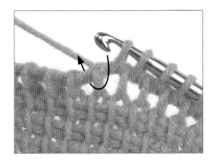

TUNISIAN DOUBLE STITCH *(abbreviated tds)*

YO, insert hook from **front** to **back** between front and back vertical bars of next stitch, YO and pull up a loop, YO and draw through 2 loops on hook *(Figs. 7a & b)*.

Fig. 7a

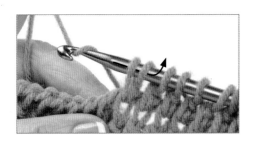

Fig. 7b

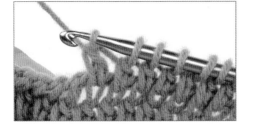

TUNISIAN BOBBLE STITCH *(abbreviated tbs)*

Inserting hook as for tks, work 3 tds in stitch indicated *(Fig. 8a)*, YO and draw through 3 loops on hook *(Fig. 8b)*. Push tbs to the **right** side.

Fig. 8a

Fig. 8b

MAKE ONE
(abbreviated M1)

Insert hook in horizontal bar before next vertical bar, YO and pull up a loop *(Fig. 9)*.

Fig. 9

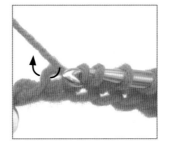

CHANGING COLORS

To change colors on the return pass, close across to last 2 stitches. Drop the old yarn and with the new yarn *(Fig. 10)*, yarn over and draw through 2 loops on hook.

Fig. 10

🎥 CROCHET STITCHES
CHAIN *(abbreviated ch)*

Bring the working yarn over the hook from **back** to **front**. Catch the yarn with the hook and turn it slightly toward you so the yarn doesn't slip off. Draw the yarn through the loop on hook *(Fig. 11)* **(first chain st made)**. Repeat for the number of chains indicated.

Fig. 11

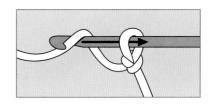

SLIP STITCH *(abbreviated slip st)*

Insert hook in stitch indicated, YO and draw through stitch and through loop on hook *(Fig. 12)*.

Fig. 12

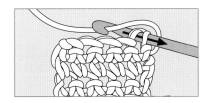

SINGLE CROCHET

(abbreviated sc)

Insert hook in stitch indicated, YO and pull up a loop, YO and draw through both loops on hook *(Fig. 13)*.

Fig. 13

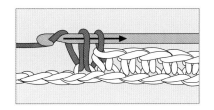

HALF DOUBLE CROCHET

(abbreviated hdc)

YO, insert hook in stitch indicated, YO and pull up a loop, YO and draw through all 3 loops on hook *(Fig. 14)*.

Fig. 14

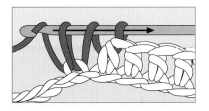

DOUBLE CROCHET

(abbreviated dc)

YO, insert hook in stitch indicated, YO and pull up a loop (3 loops on hook), YO and draw through 2 loops on hook *(Fig. 15a)*, YO and draw through remaining 2 loops on hook *(Fig. 15b)*.

Fig. 15a

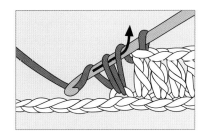

Fig. 15b

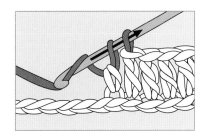

JOINING WITH SC

When instructed to join with sc, begin with a slip knot on hook. Insert hook in stitch indicated, YO and pull up a loop, YO and draw through both loops on hook *(Figs. 16a & b)*.

Fig. 16a   Fig. 16b

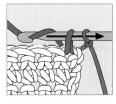 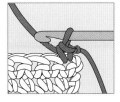

MEET
Sharon Silverman

Sharon Hernes Silverman's fresh designs and crystal-clear instructions have made her books and patterns favorites among crocheters. A former travel writer, writing instructor, and restaurant reviewer, Silverman is based in West Chester, Pennsylvania. She blogs at www.SharonSilverman.com and maintains an active presence on Facebook and Ravelry. She is a professional member of the Crochet Guild of America (CGOA) and a design member of The National NeedleArts Association (TNNA). Silverman and her husband are the parents of two college age sons. Although Silverman is a lifelong crafter who has done everything from needlepoint to candle-making, her true passion is for Tunisian crochet.

Yarn Information

The Baby Blankets in this book were made using Light Weight or Medium Weight yarn. Any brand of Light Weight or Medium Weight yarn may be used. It is best to refer to the yardage/meters when determining how many balls or skeins to purchase. Remember, to arrive at the finished size, it is the GAUGE/TENSION that is important, not the brand of yarn.

For your convenience, listed below are the specific yarns used to create our photography models.

BASKET WEAVE BLOCKS
Bernat® Softee® Baby™
Blue - #02002 Pale Blue
Lt Blue - #30300 Baby Denim Marl

PURPLE GARDEN
Red Heart® With Love™
#1816 Waterlily

FROSTED STITCH STRIPES
Red Heart® Soft Baby Steps®
Green - #9620 Baby Green
Yellow - #9200 Baby Yellow

COLOR WAVES
Red Heart® Soft®
Green - #4420 Guacamole
White - #4600 White
Purple - #3720 Lavender
Lt Purple - #9520 Lilac

BUBBLING BOBBLES
Red Heart® Soft Baby Steps®
White - #9600 White
Yellow - #9200 Baby Yellow
Green - #9620 Baby Green

TELEGRAM
Red Heart® Baby TLC
White - #5011 White
Blue - #5935 Clear Blue

CABLES & HONEYCOMBS
Lion Brand® Vanna's Choice® Baby
#098 Lamb

BRIGHT STRANDS
Red Heart® Classic™
White - #0001 White
Blue - #0853 Soft Navy
Yellow - #0230 Yellow

We have made every effort to ensure that these instructions are accurate and complete. We cannot, however, be responsible for human error, typographical mistakes, or variations in individual work.

Production Team: Instructional/Technical Editor - Lois J. Long; Editorial Writer - Susan Frantz Wiles; Senior Graphic Artist - Lora Puls; Graphic Artist - Kara Darling; Photo Stylist - Lori Wenger; and Photographers - Jason Masters and Mark Mathews.